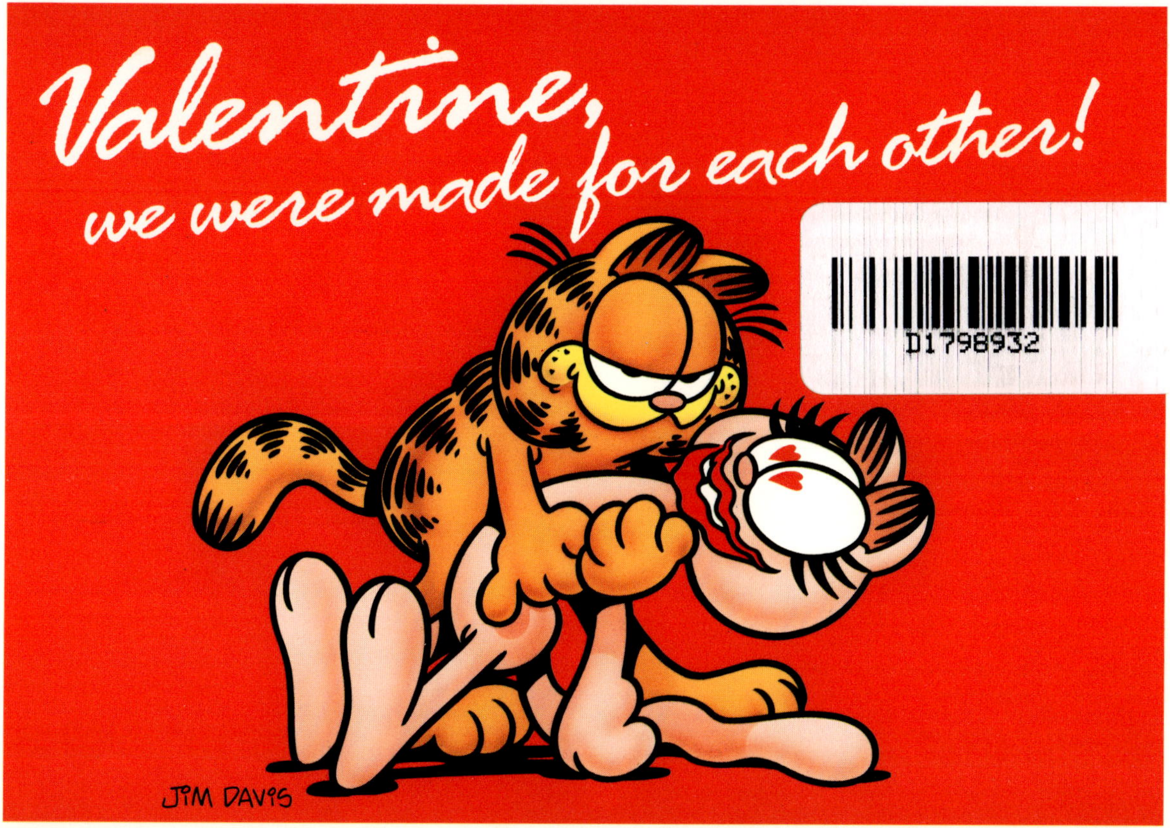
Valentine,
we were made for each other!
JIM DAVIS

Ballantine Books • New York
Illustration by Jim Davis

Hold me! Kiss me!

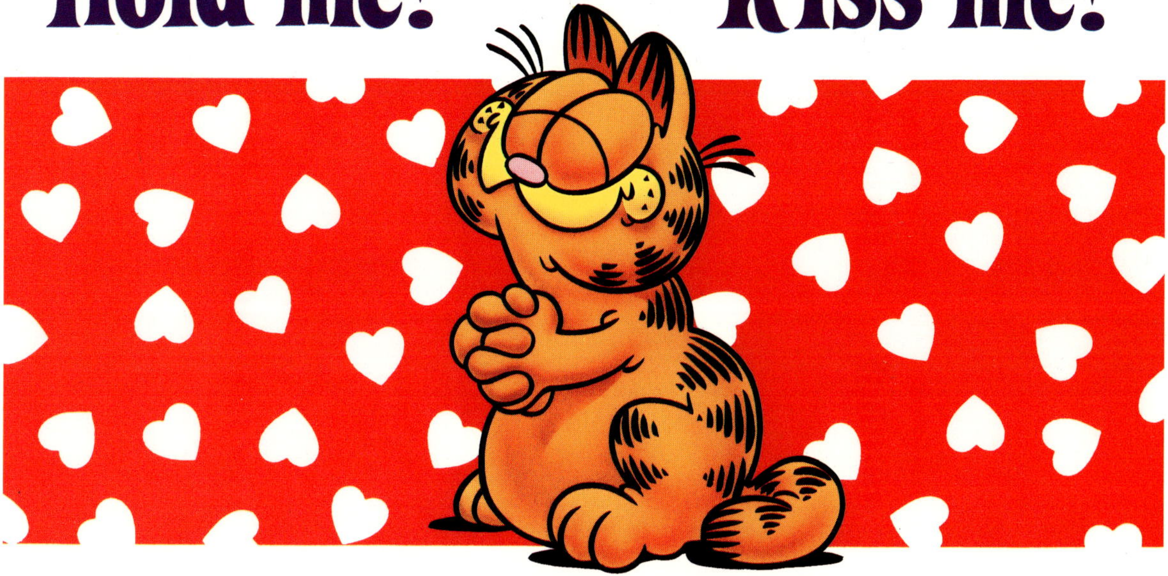

Make me eat chocolate!

Ballantine Books • New York
Illustration by Jim Davis

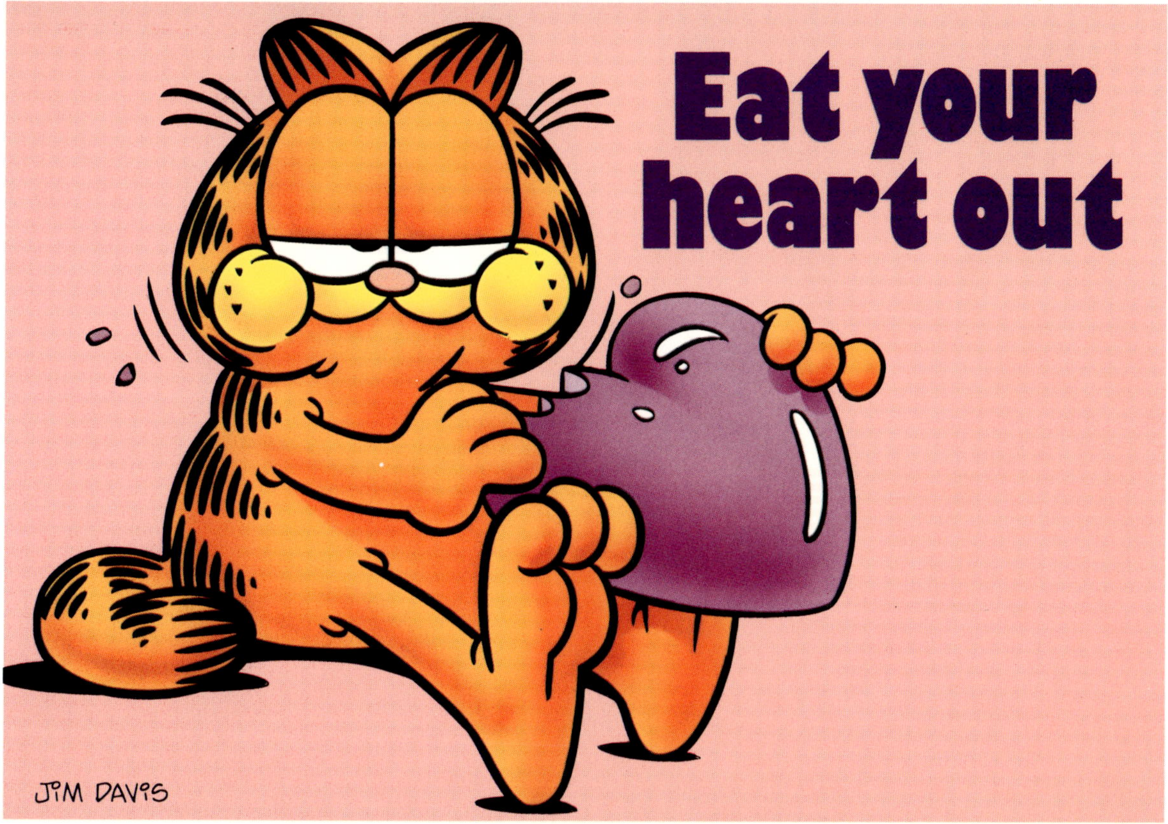
Eat your heart out
JIM DAVIS

Ballantine Books • New York
Illustration by Jim Davis

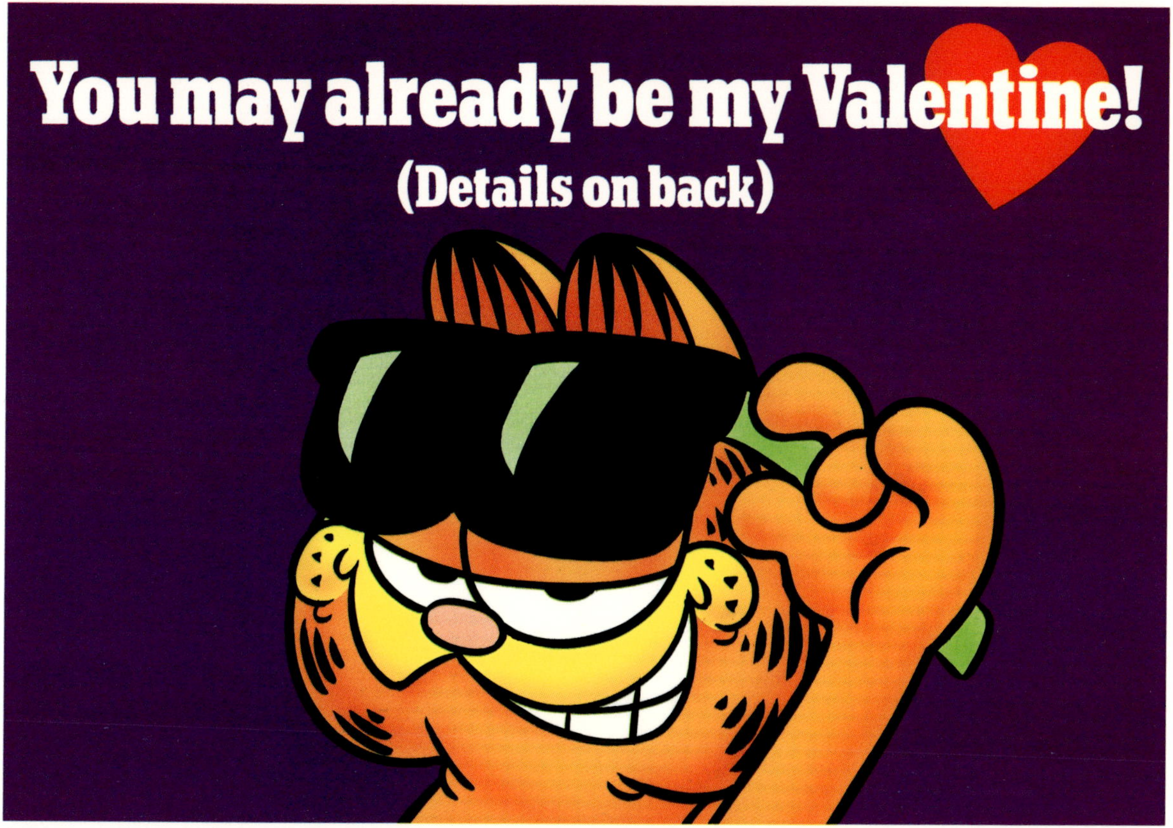
You may already be my Valentine!
(Details on back)

Ballantine Books • New York
Illustration by Jim Davis

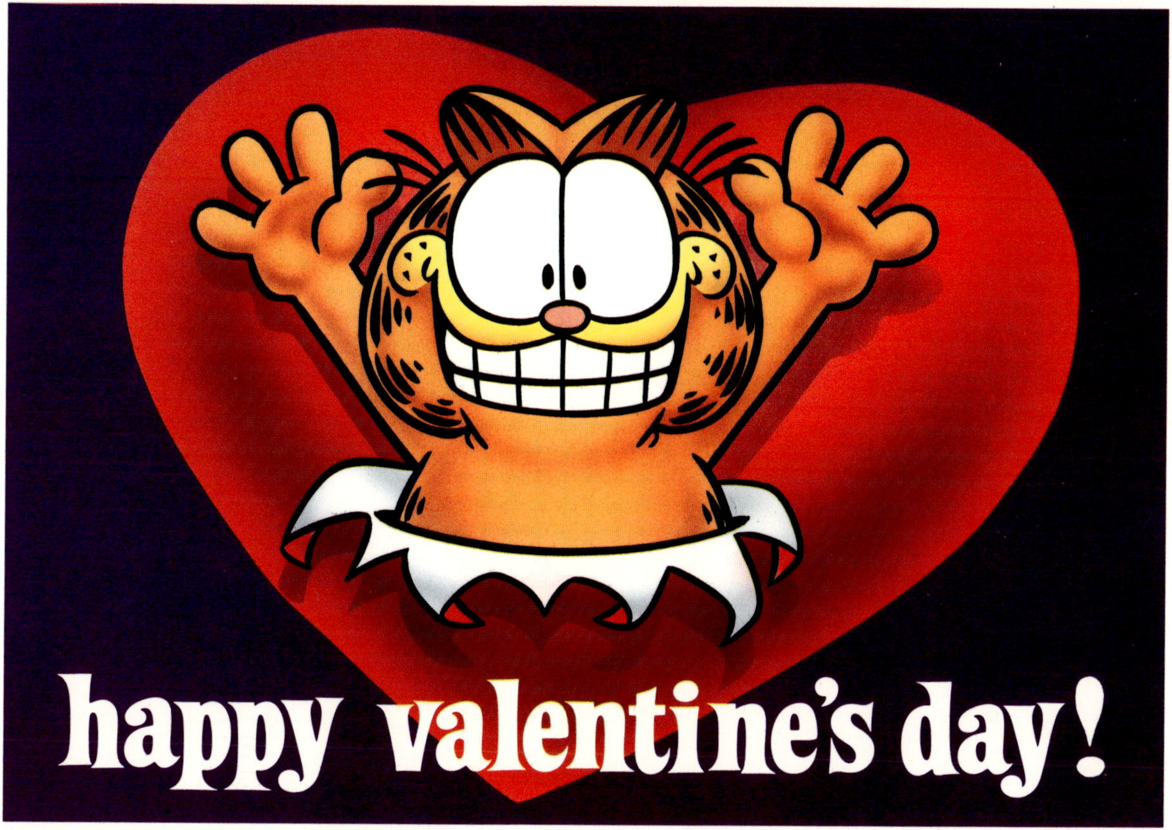
happy valentine's day!

Ballantine Books • New York
Illustration by Jim Davis

For you on this Valentine's day, I've set my lips on STUN!

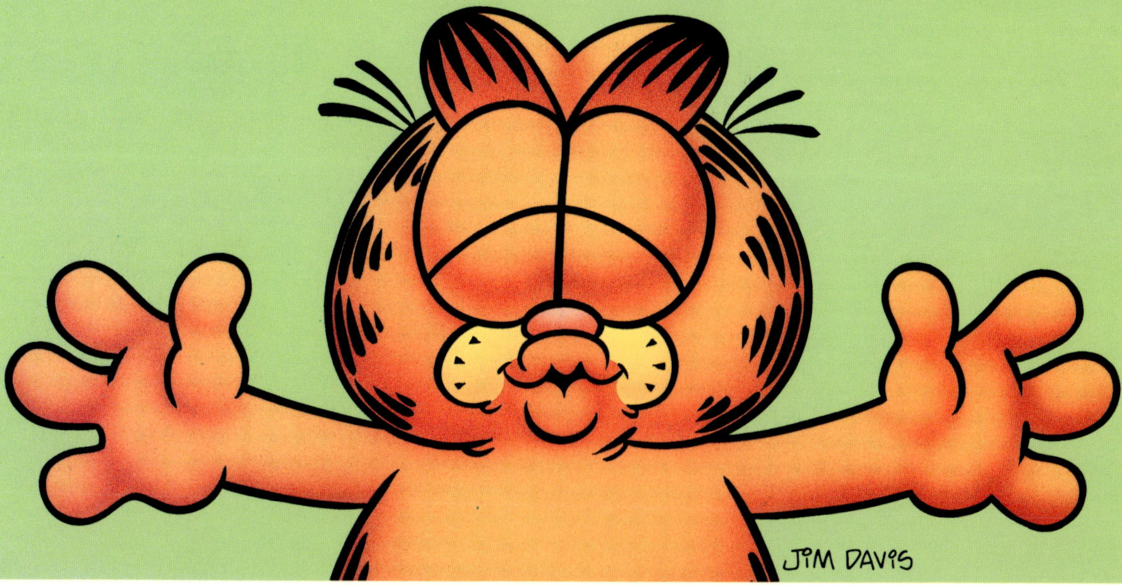
JIM DAVIS

Ballantine Books • New York
Illustration by Jim Davis

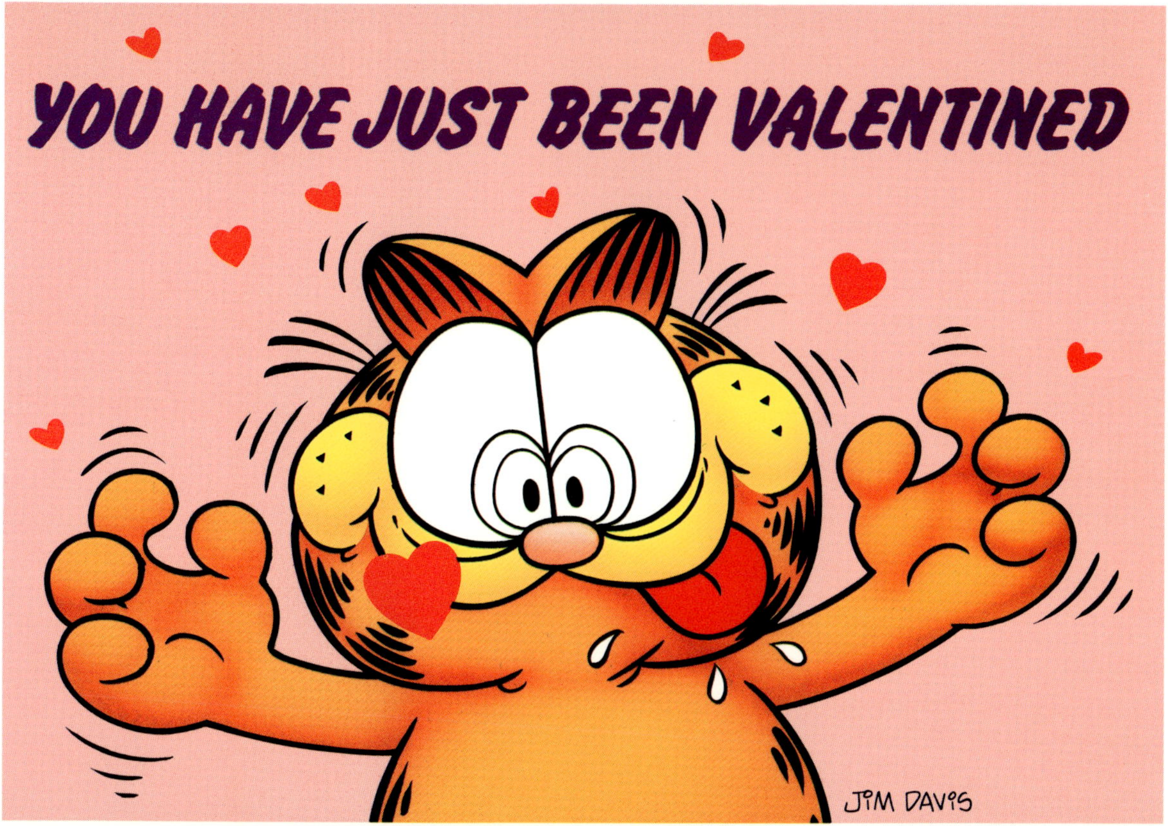
YOU HAVE JUST BEEN VALENTINED
JIM DAVIS

Ballantine Books • New York
Illustration by Jim Davis

I knocked myself out for your Valentine

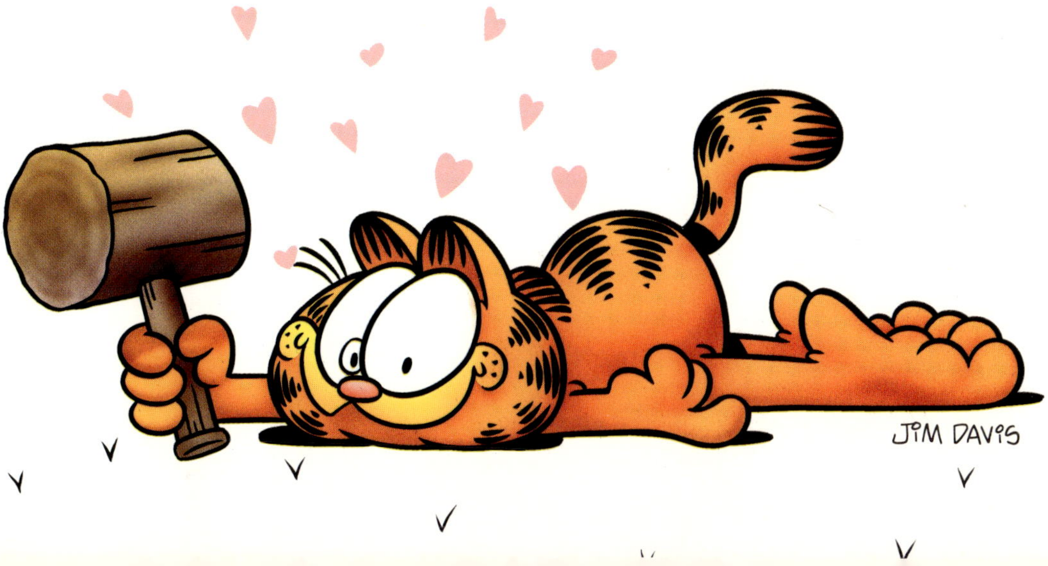
JIM DAVIS

Ballantine Books • New York
Illustration by Jim Davis

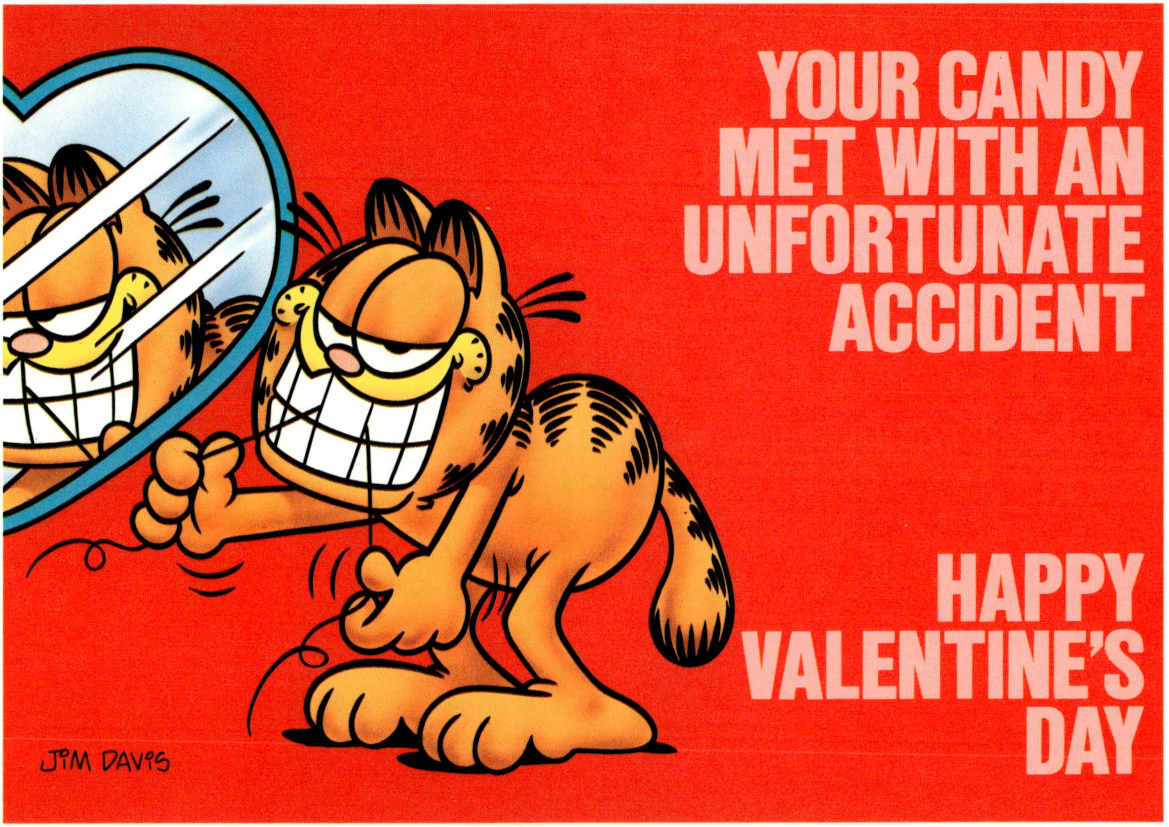
JIM DAVIS

YOUR CANDY
MET WITH AN
UNFORTUNATE
ACCIDENT

HAPPY
VALENTINE'S
DAY

Ballantine Books • New York
Illustration by Jim Davis

READ MY LIPS

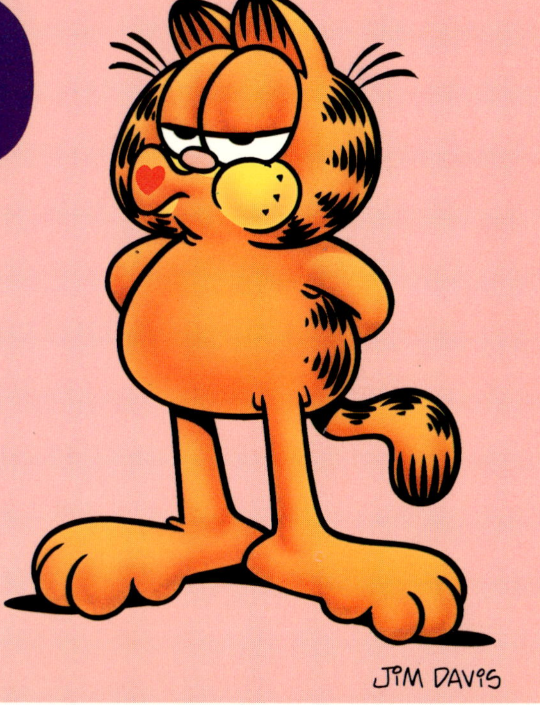
JIM DAVIS

Ballantine Books • New York
Illustration by Jim Davis

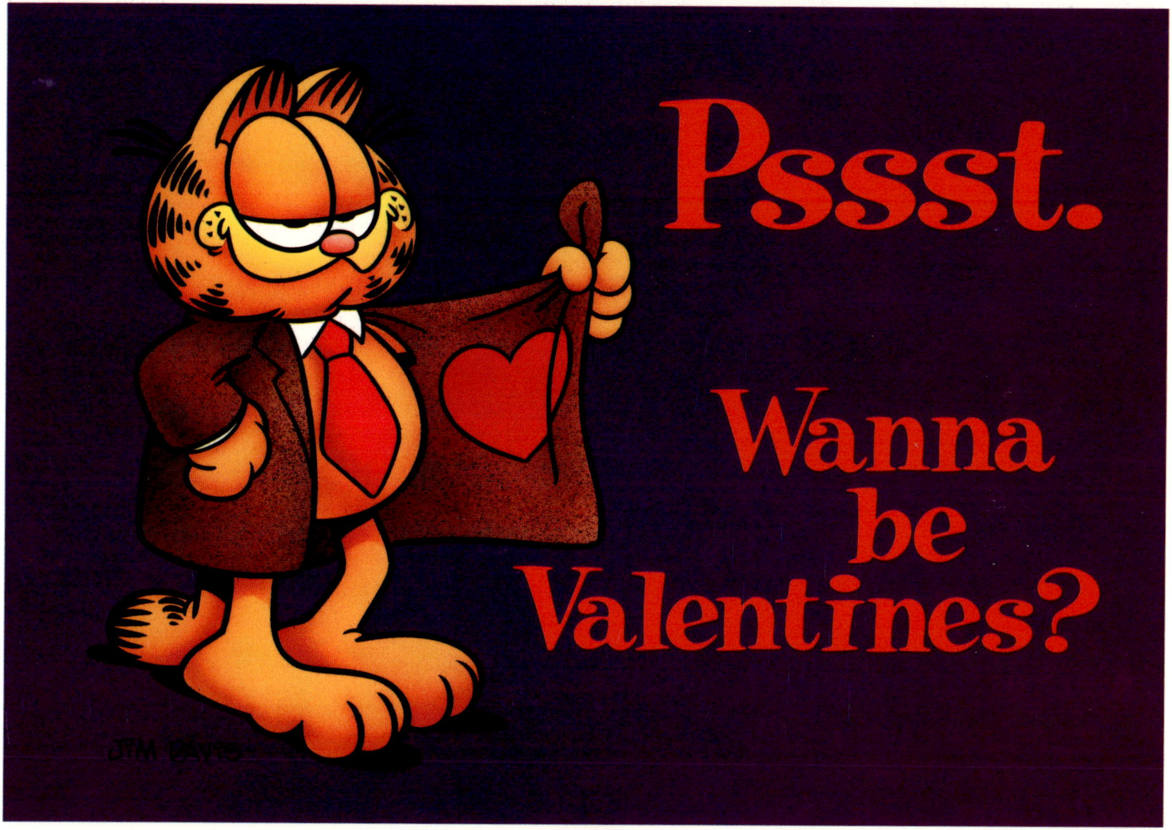
Pssst.
Wanna be Valentines?
JIM DAVIS

Ballantine Books • New York
Illustration by Jim Davis

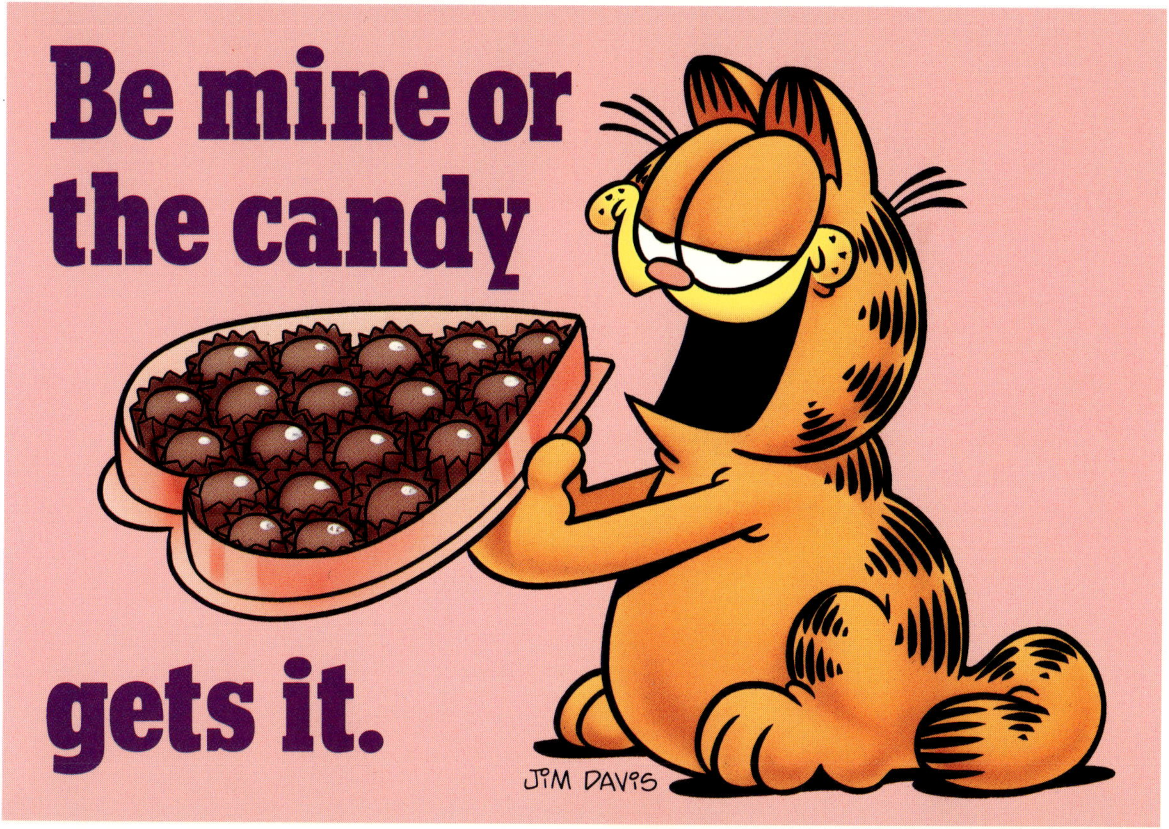
Be mine or
the candy
gets it.
JIM DAVIS

Ballantine Books • New York
Illustration by Jim Davis

BE MINE OR I'LL BUST!

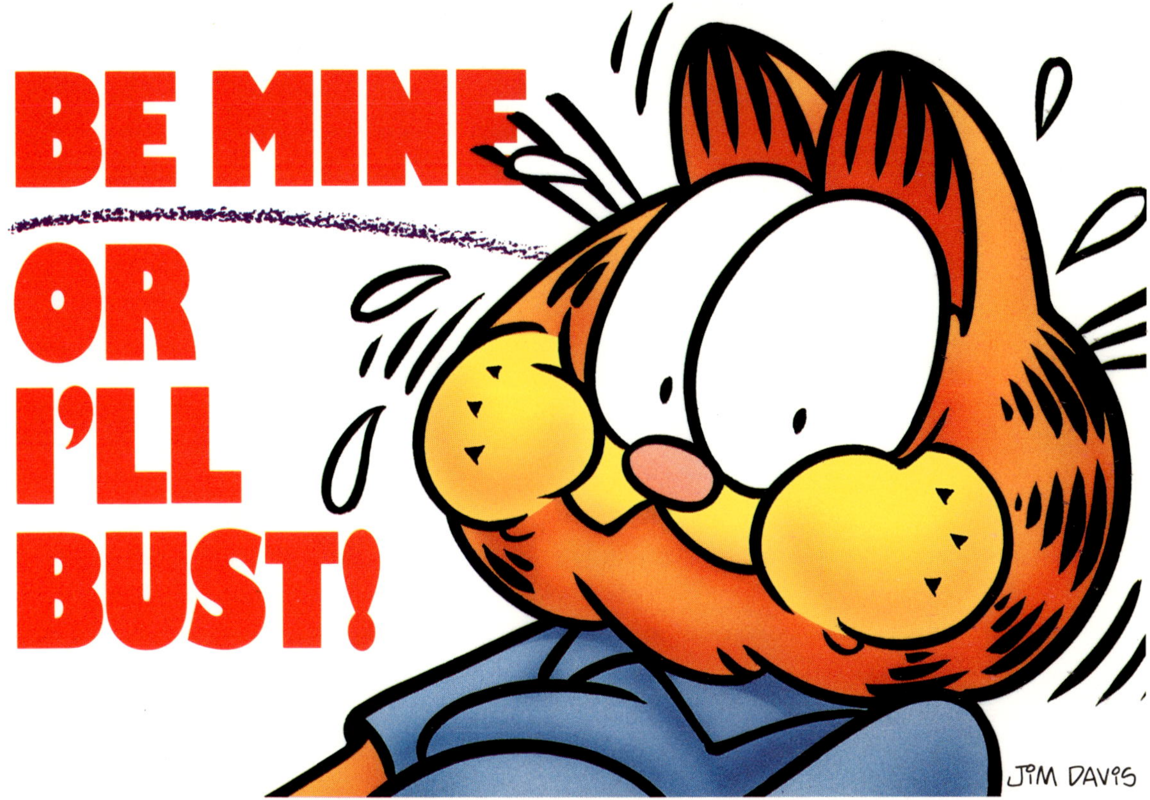
JIM DAVIS

Ballantine Books • New York
Illustration by Jim Davis

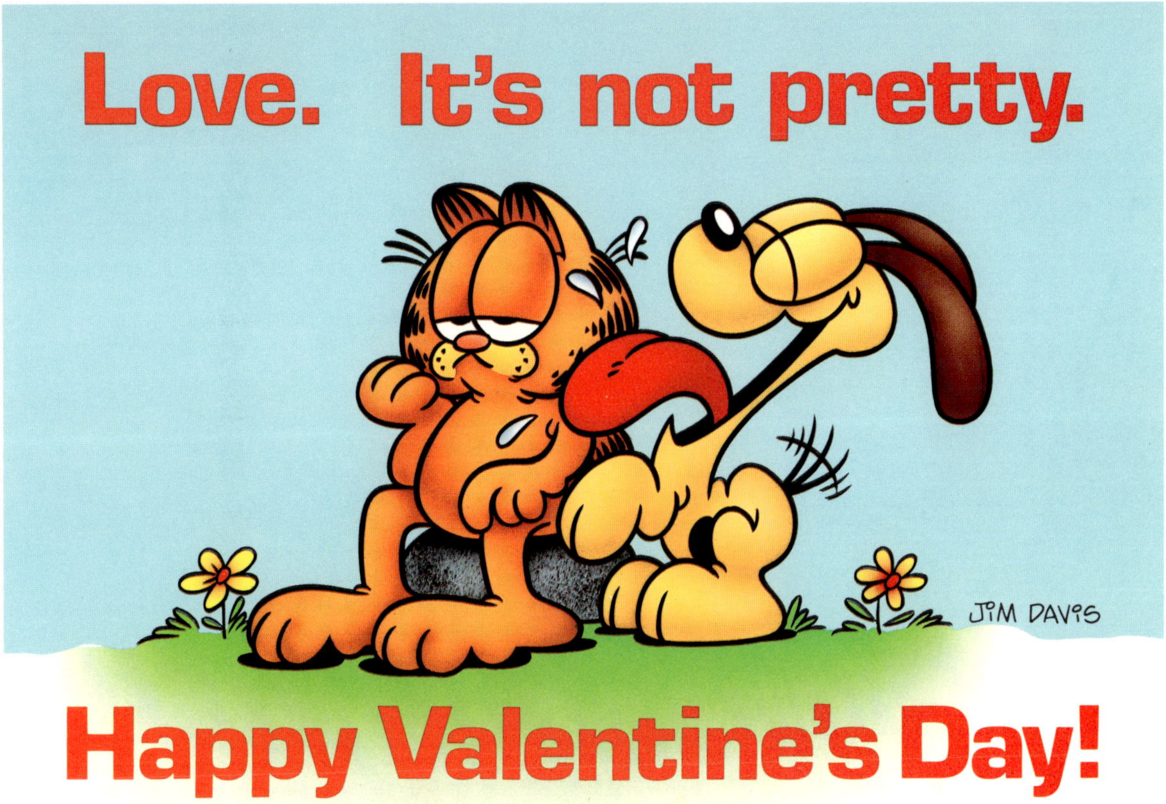
Love. It's not pretty.
JIM DAVIS
Happy Valentine's Day!

Ballantine Books • New York
Illustration by Jim Davis

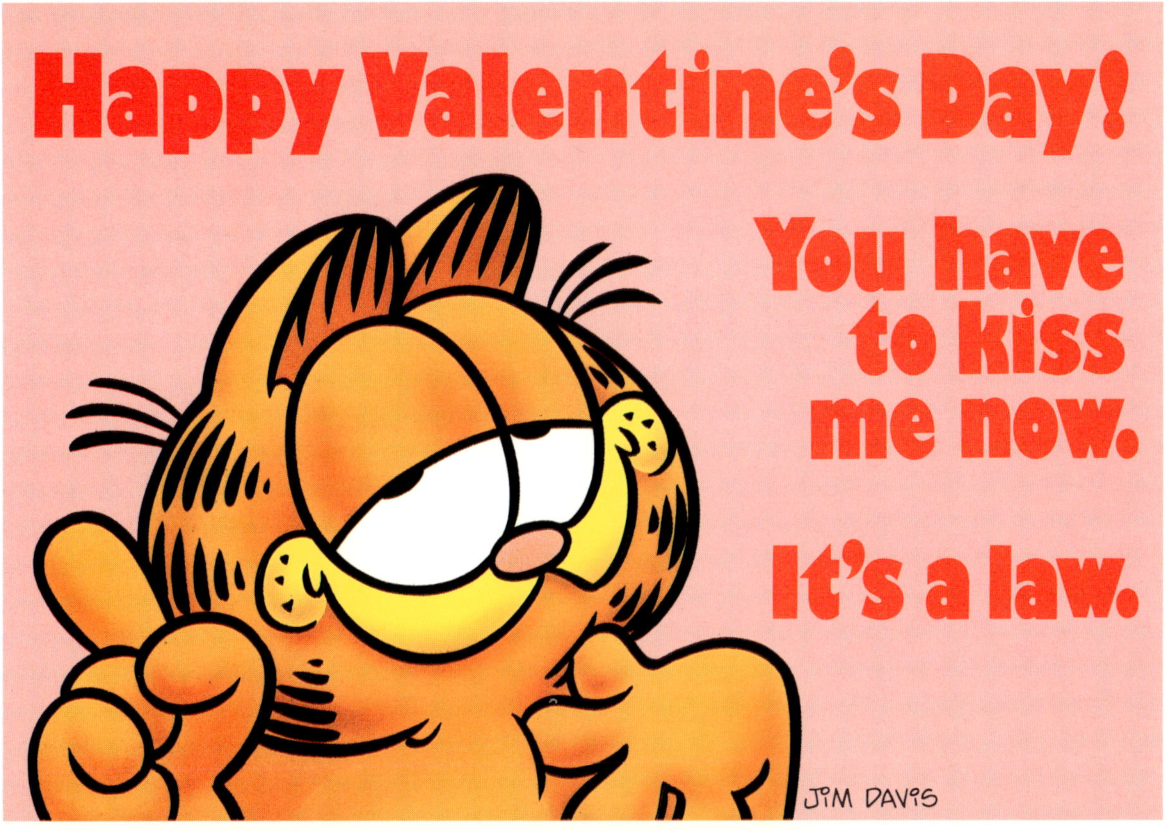
Happy Valentine's Day!
You have to kiss me now.
It's a law.
JIM DAVIS

Ballantine Books • New York
Illustration by Jim Davis

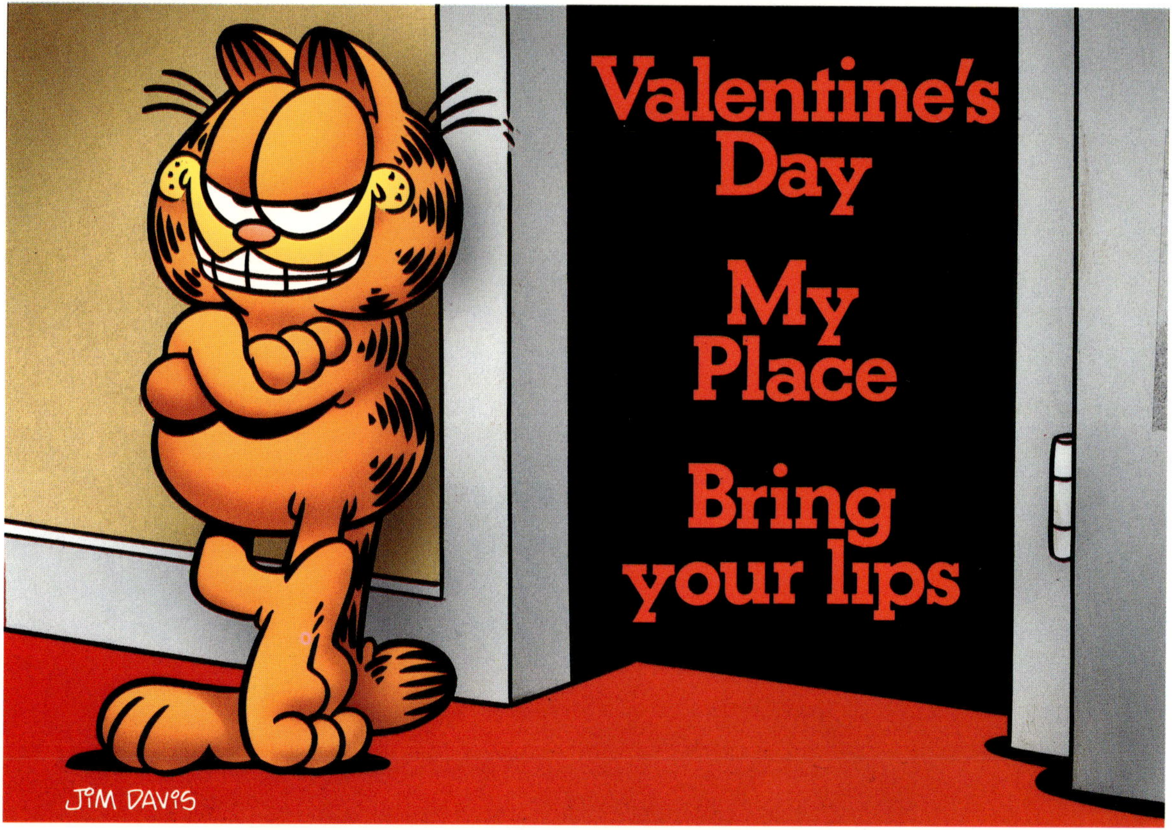
Valentine's Day
My Place
Bring your lips
JIM DAVIS

Ballantine Books • New York

Illustration by Jim Davis

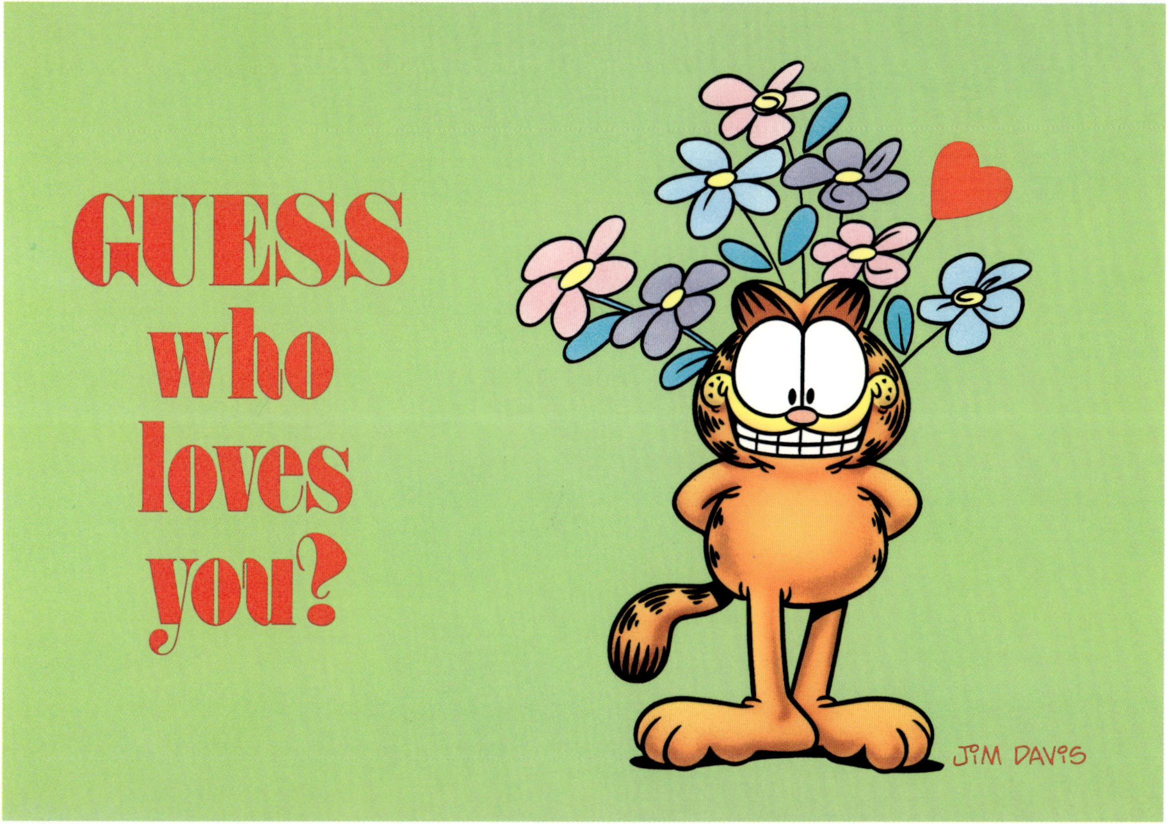
GUESS who loves you?
JIM DAVIS

Ballantine Books • New York
Illustration by Jim Davis

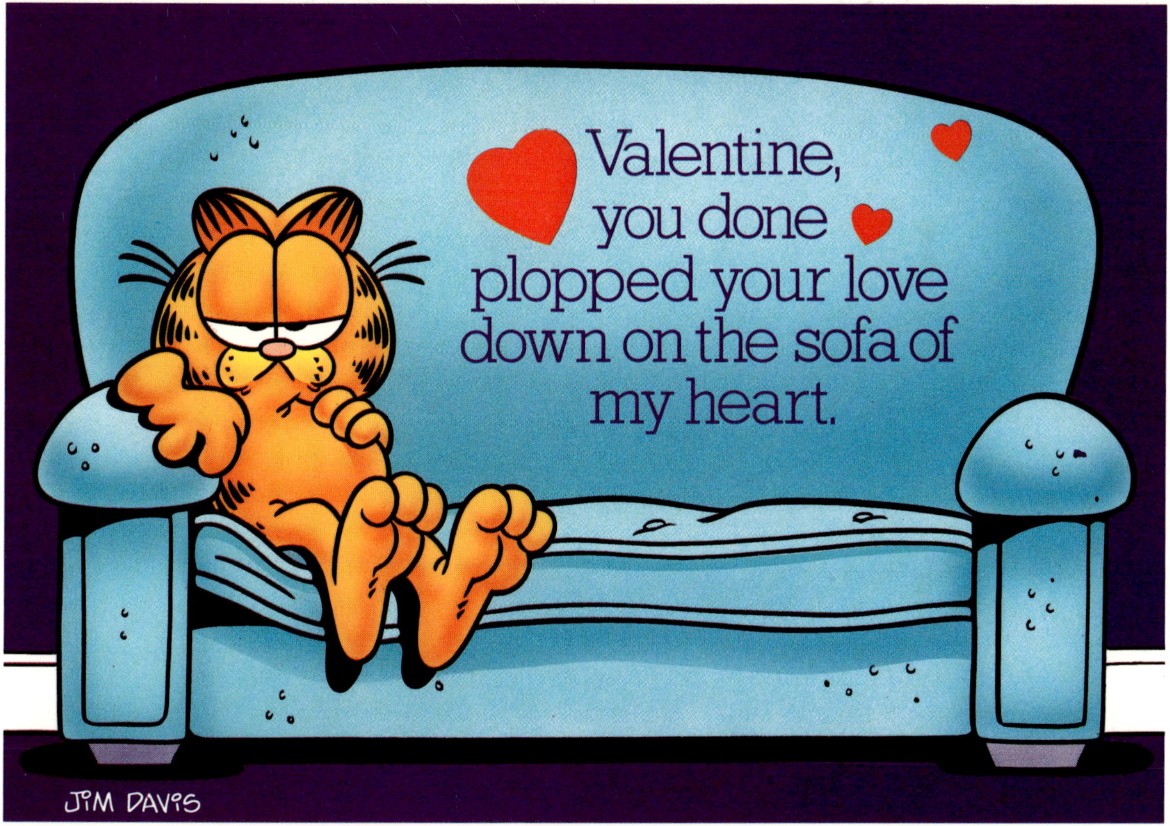
Valentine,
you done
plopped your love
down on the sofa of
my heart.
JIM DAVIS

Ballantine Books • New York
Illustration by Jim Davis

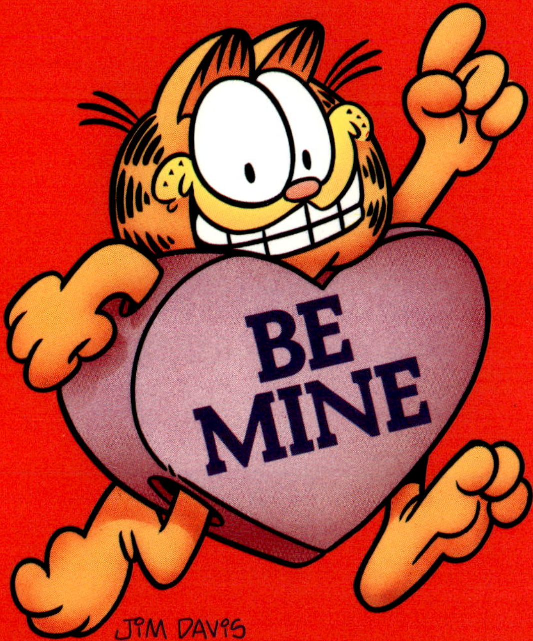
BE MINE
JIM DAVIS

I'M YOUR
REAL
VALENTINE

ALL OTHERS
ARE
CHEAP
IMITATIONS

Ballantine Books • New York
Illustration by Jim Davis

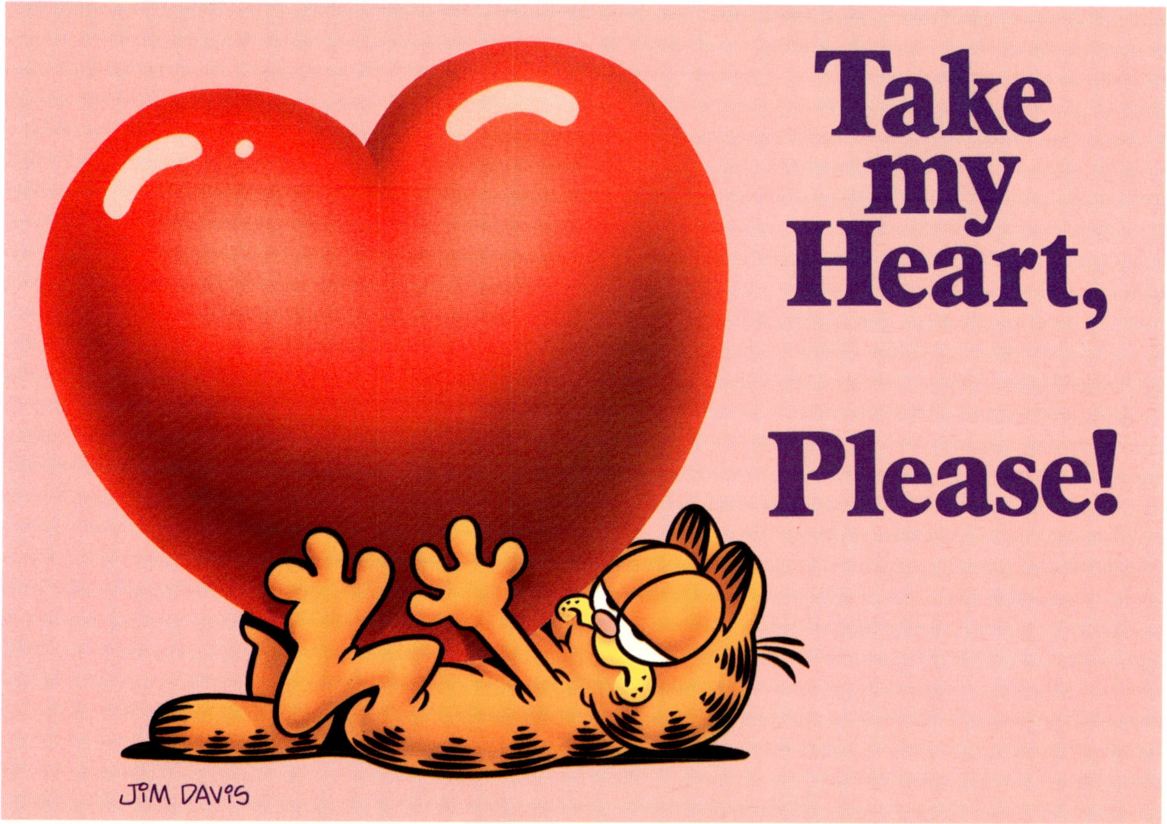
Take my Heart,
Please!
JIM DAVIS

Ballantine Books • New York
Illustration by Jim Davis

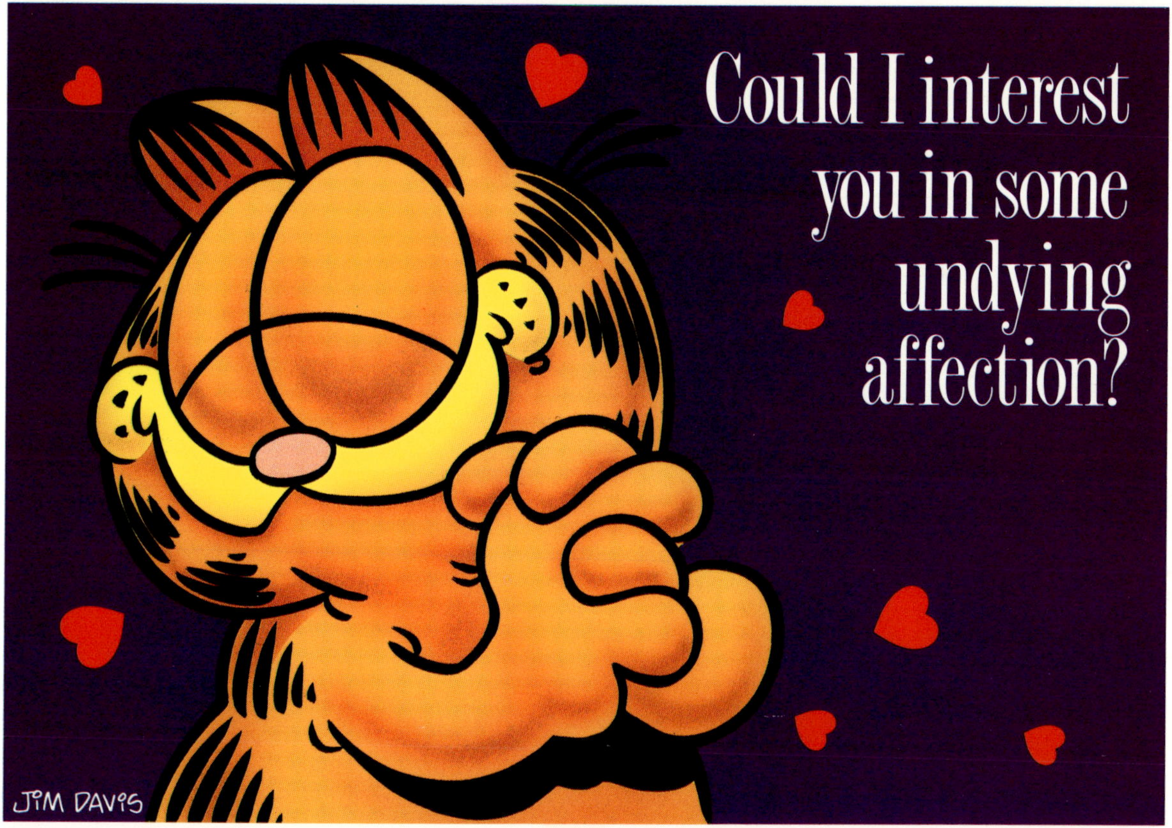
Could I interest you in some undying affection?
JIM DAVIS

Ballantine Books • New York
Illustration by Jim Davis

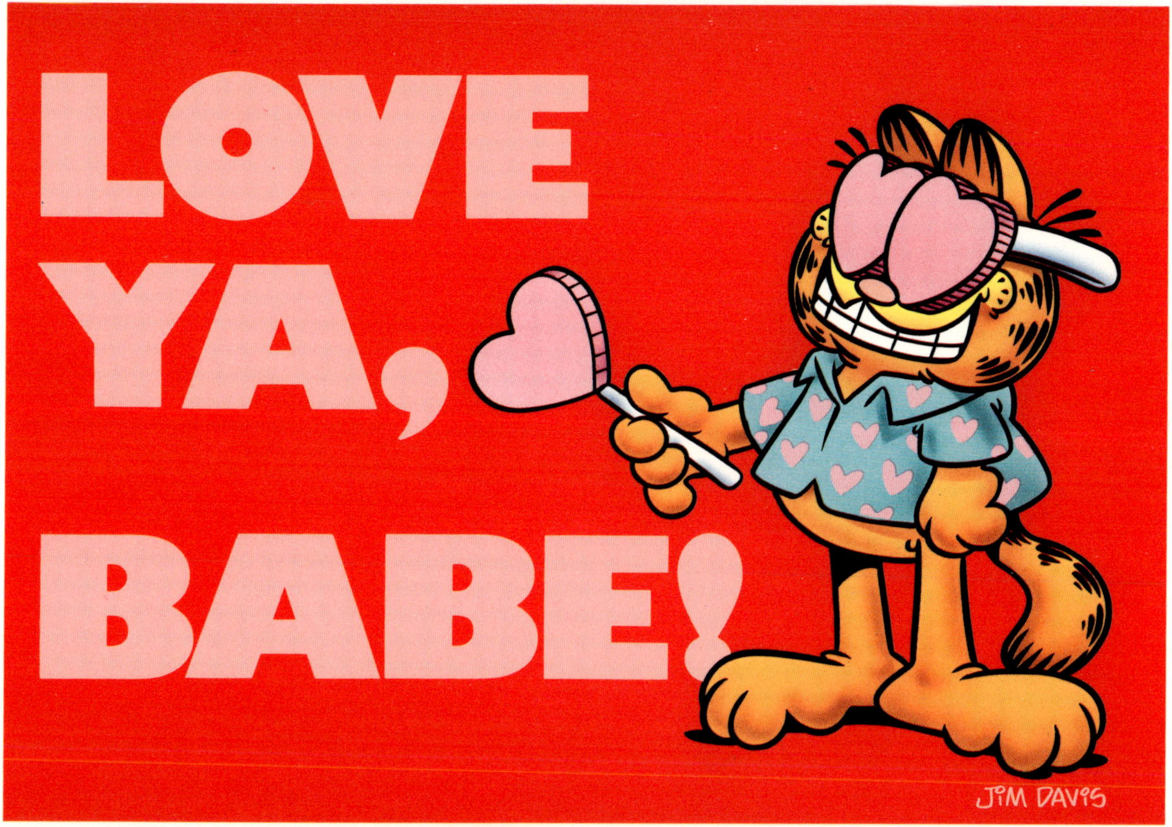
LOVE YA, BABE!
JIM DAVIS

Ballantine Books • New York
Illustration by Jim Davis

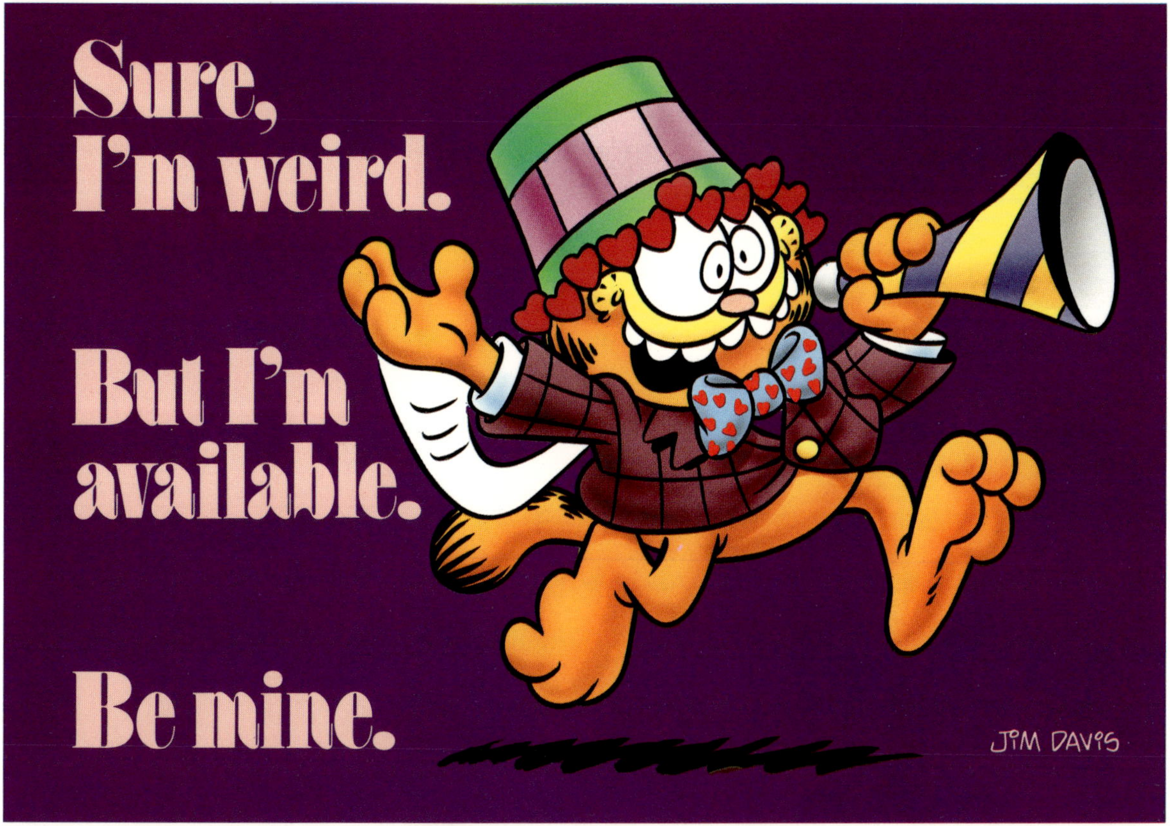
Sure, I'm weird.
But I'm available.
Be mine.
JIM DAVIS

Ballantine Books • New York
Illustration by Jim Davis

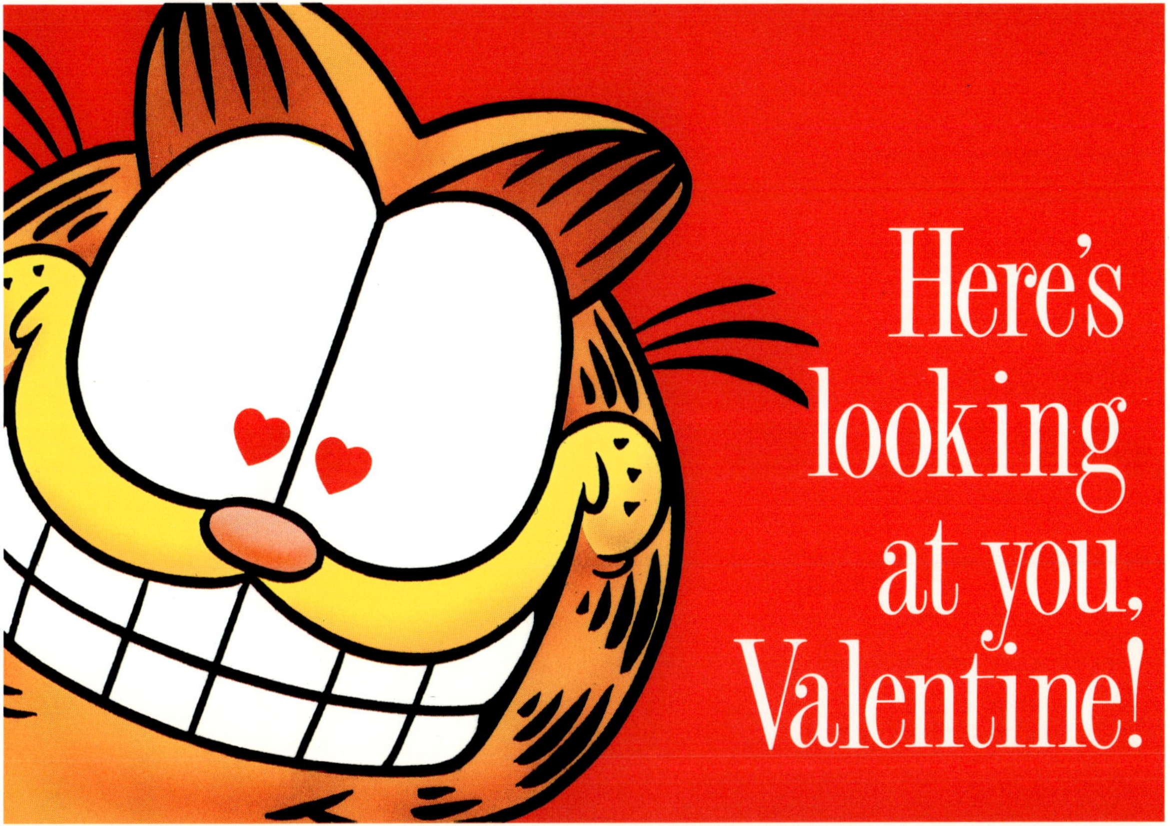

Here's looking at you, Valentine!

Ballantine Books • New York
Illustration by Jim Davis

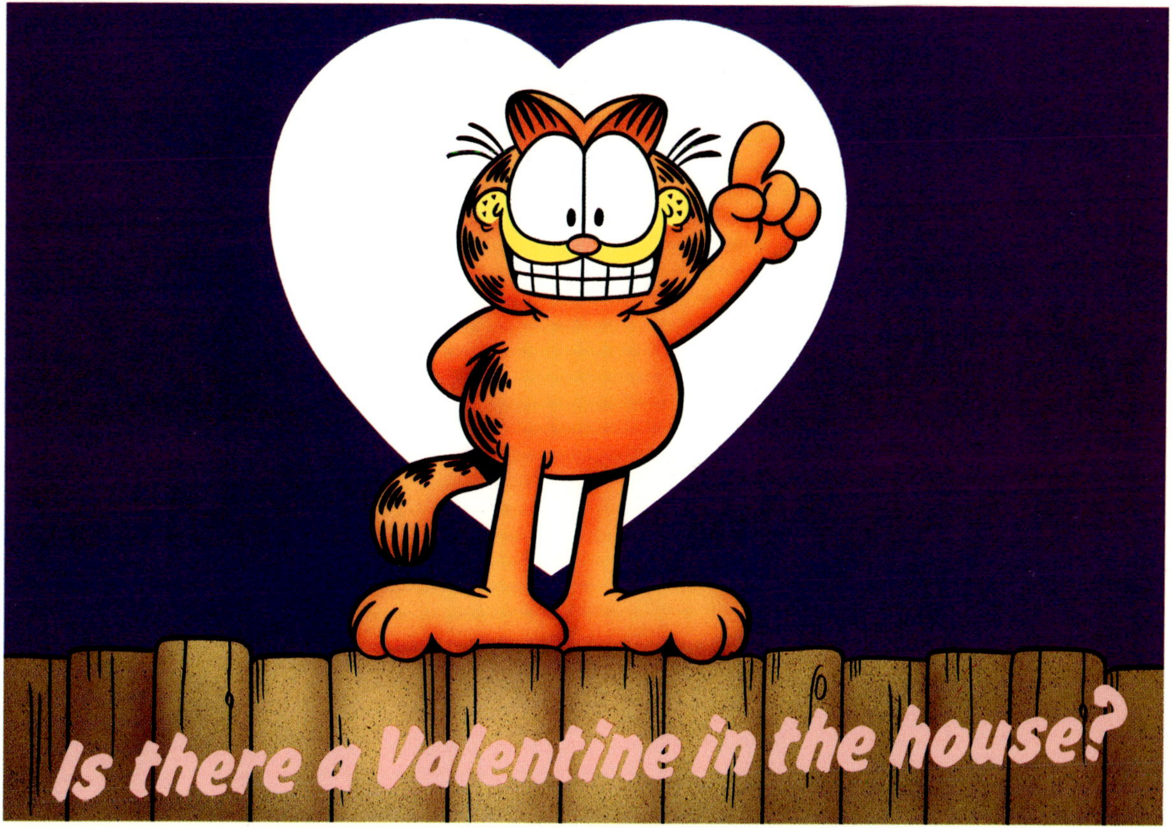
Is there a Valentine in the house?

Ballantine Books • New York
Illustration by Jim Davis

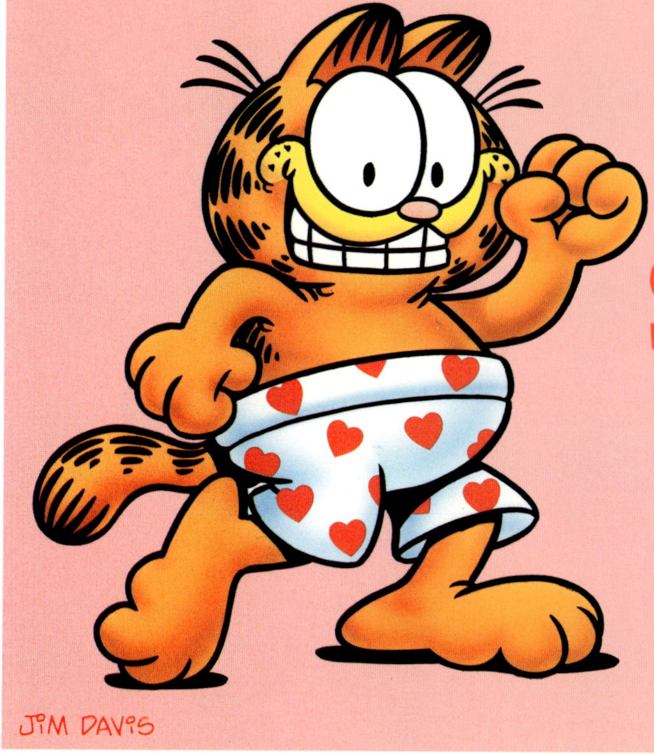
JIM DAVIS

Read my Shorts...

and have a happy Valentine's Day

Ballantine Books • New York
Illustration by Jim Davis

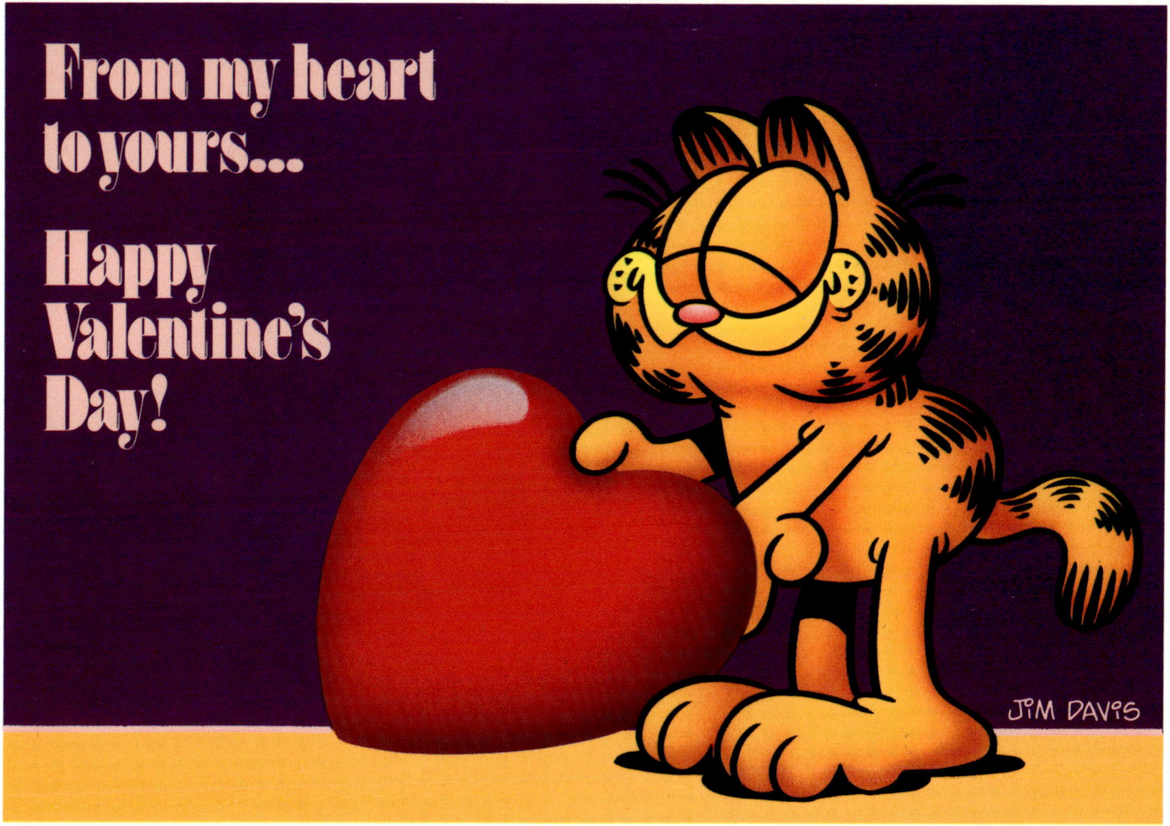
From my heart
to yours...
Happy
Valentine's
Day!
JIM DAVIS

Ballantine Books • New York

Illustration by Jim Davis

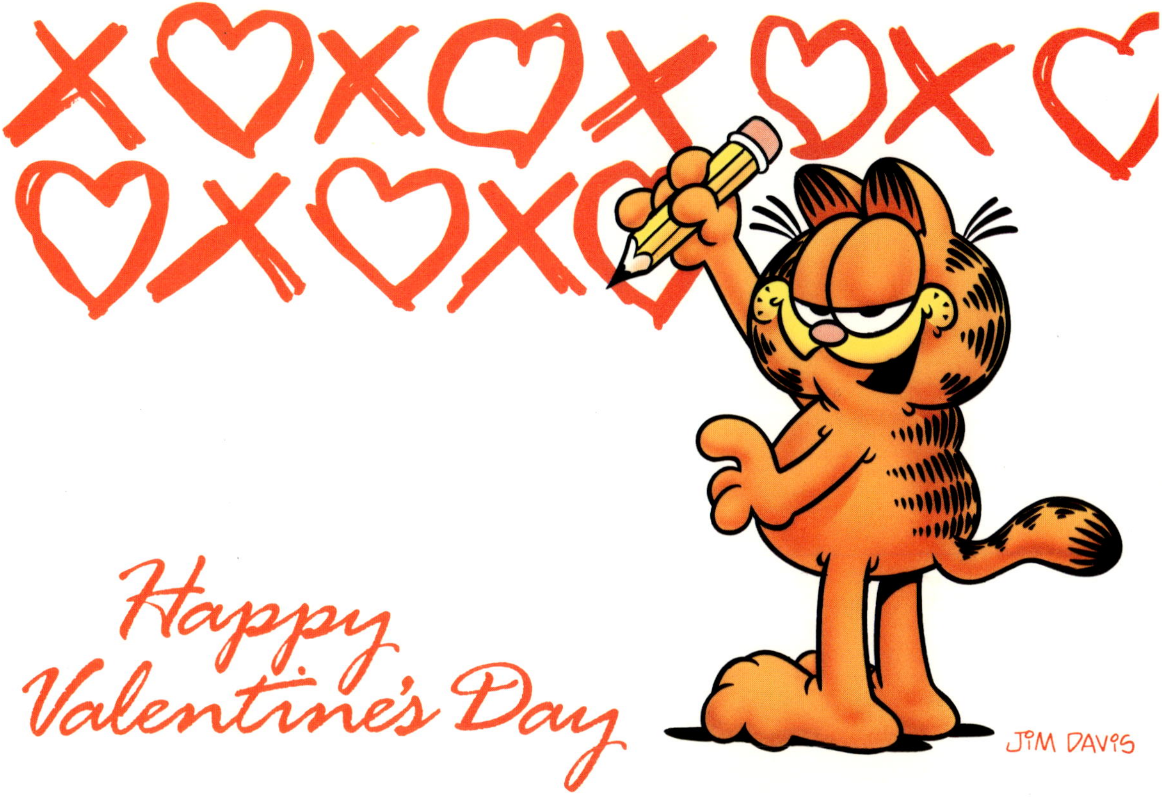
Happy
Valentine's Day
JIM DAVIS

Ballantine Books • New York
Illustration by Jim Davis

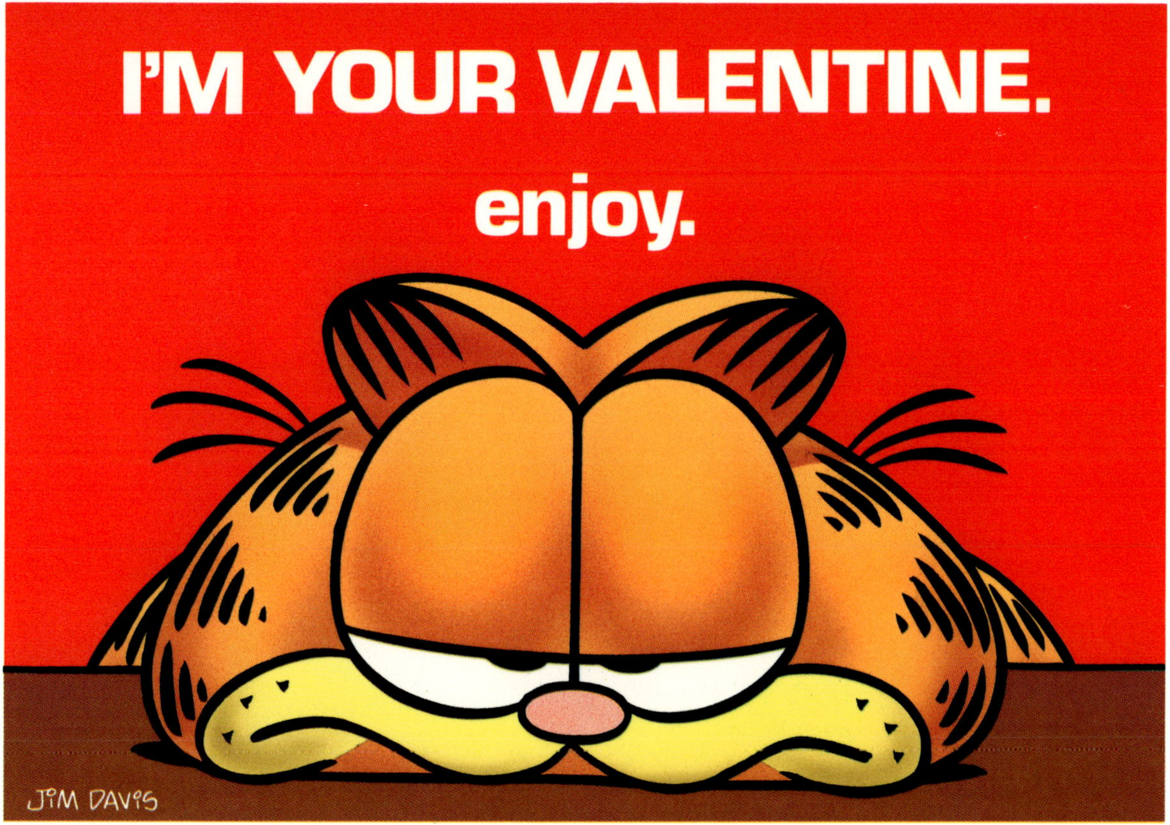
I'M YOUR VALENTINE.
enjoy.
JIM DAVIS

Ballantine Books • New York
Illustration by Jim Davis

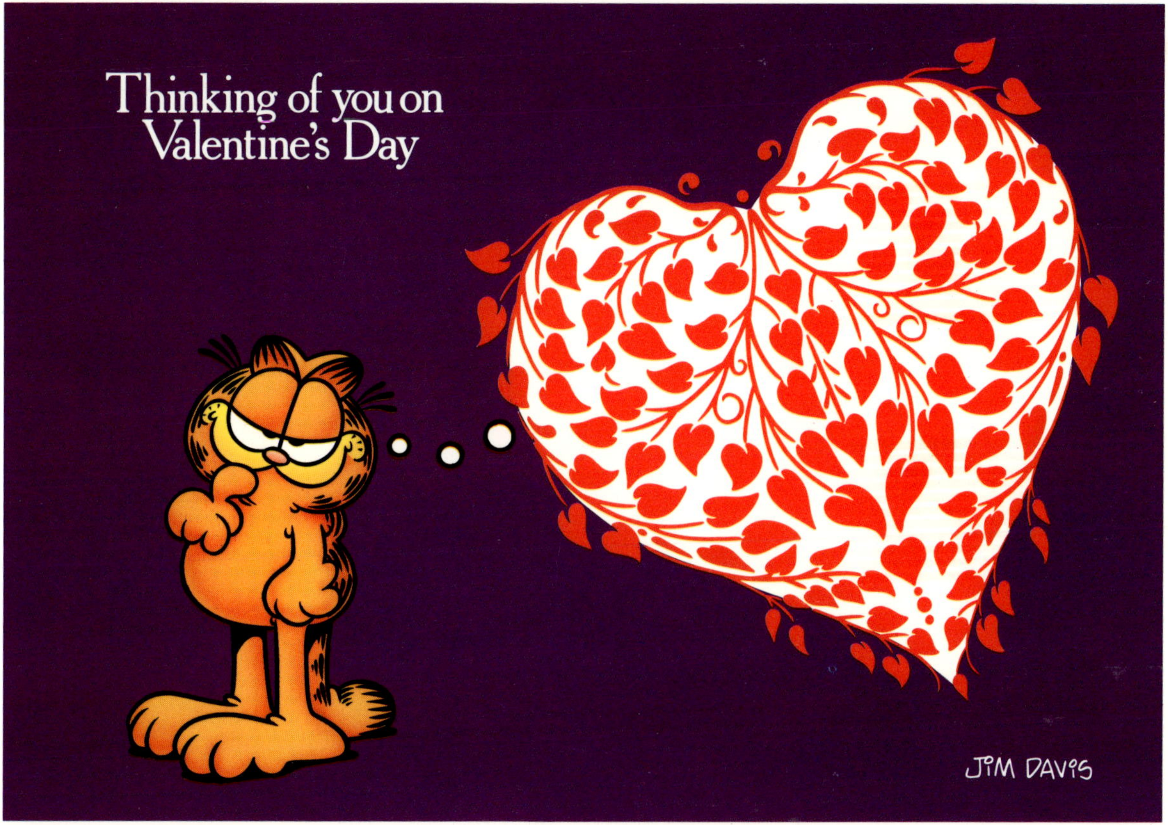
Thinking of you on
Valentine's Day
JIM DAVIS

Ballantine Books • New York
Illustration by Jim Davis